Prayers for Priests

Prayers for Priests

and Those Who Pray for Them

Rev. T. Ronald Haney

With Illustrations by
Bro. Michael O'Neill McGrath, OSFS

A Crossroad Faith & Formation Book
The Crossroad Publishing Company
New York

The Crossroad Publishing Company
370 Lexington Avenue, New York, NY 10017

Printed in the United States of America

Library of Congress Cataloging-in-Publication Data

Haney, Thomas R.
Prayer for priests / by T. Ronald Haney : with illustrations by Michael O'Neill McGrath.
p. cm.
Includes bibliographical references.
ISBN 1-8245-1816-0 (hardcover)
1. Prayers for clergy. 2. Catholic Church – Clergy Prayer-books and devotions – English. I. Title.
BV283.C47H35 1999
242′.892–dc21 99-23018

1 2 3 4 5 6 7 8 9 10 04 03 02 01 00 99

Although these prayers are for those of the ordained priesthood, my hope is that all who believe that they have been baptized into Jesus' priesthood will find help and enlightenment in them.

Contents

Part One
SCRIPTURAL INTERCESSIONS

Part Two
SAINTLY INTERCESSIONS

Part One

SCRIPTURAL INTERCESSIONS

1

Indwelling Trinity – One Me

Indwelling Trinity,
Father, Son, and Spirit,
infinite, all-powerful, eternal,
all-knowing, all-loving God,
I believe with all the sincerity of my faith
that you are dwelling within me,
closer to me than I am to myself.

As I go within myself
and dwell within you within me,
I thank you again for the precious gift of my priesthood
and recognize my unworthiness.
Yet I believe wholeheartedly
that you have enhanced my worth
with this sacramental gift.

In your presence within me,
all-knowing Trinity, Father, Son, and Spirit,
I can only be my real self:
no masks, no pretenses,
no disguises, no rationalizations,
no fake-outs,
no dissimulations,
no chicanery.

Here within you dwelling within me,
I am like Adam and Eve before the Fall:
stripped naked,
not physically but spiritually,
psychologically, and emotionally.

There are so many times when appearances
take on a life of their own in my priestly ministry:
I may be feeling as low as an outgoing tide
but I have to appear cheerful and optimistic
because someone is pouring out a mouthful
of pain-filled heartbreaks.

Or I may be senselessly agitated because right before Mass
someone has accosted me about some incidental.
Yet I must appear before the people as totally focused
and filled with faith and love
to challenge them to worship in spirit and truth.

But here and now, Trinity within me, I am me.
I may have arrived in your presence with a lot of baggage
like agitation or a downer,
but you within me somehow enable me
to transform these burdens into packages
of conversational prayer.

I think back now to the times when I feel down and out
because I seemed to have failed someone
who came to me seeking guidance and direction.

Was my apparent failure due to the weakness of my insights
or to the blindness of that person's sight?
I'm never sure.
How much do I have to give?
How disposed is the seeker to receive?

Here within you within me,
I ponder my need to rest
in the mystery of human communication.

This person who has come to me for help
walks in and out of my life,
leaving me to stalk her memory.
I pray for her, but I never hear from her again.
My telephone messages go unanswered.
I am left with the cataclysmic feeling of failure.

And so here I am.
In your presence within me.
I listen.
You will speak to me.
This I believe.
I let go of my problem,
of my feeling of failure.
I dwell within you.
Speak to me.
Give me hope that I may not allow my failings to cripple me
for the many short races I must run in my priestly ministry.
Enlighten the faith consciousness I bring to you,
indwelling Lover.

2

Unknown Reaper – Sow Me

Jesus, my indwelling friend,
I have listened,
and you have spoken to me.

I am exhilarated because your words tell me
that my failures are opportunities to move forward.

"One sows, another reaps."

I no longer have to sink into the swamp of discouragement
because I have apparently failed to help someone
or preach effectively
or make vital connections
between what I believe and how I live.
I am primarily a sower of seeds.

If I am going to maintain
a hope-filled optimism about my priestly ministry,
I need to recognize with zestful faith
that I am not a hunter of results,
especially immediate results
that bolster my ego
rather than deepen my humility
at the precious gift of priesthood you have given me.

Loving Indweller,
I am a sower.
Perhaps years from now, someone else will come after me
and gather the harvest from the seeds I have scattered,
just as the harvest I am now reaping
is the result of the work
of someone who came before me.
It is the mystery of ministry.
"One sows, another reaps."

Eternal Father, dwelling within me,
there are times when I get so discouraged.
I try but so often it seems it's to no avail.

There are the challenges
like guiding someone out of a stony feeling of grudgebearing,
but the person refuses to let go.
Or I attempt to give guidance to a couple
who are caught in the quicksand of a problem,
and they sit and stare at me like two mannequins.
Or I try to console parents whose little child has just died,
and my words seem to float off beyond their hearing.

Help me to overcome discouragement
by continually meditating on Jesus' words,
"One sows, another reaps."

These words are or should be the touchstone of all my efforts.

Indwelling Trinity,
I want to enter fully into this mystery of seed-sowing.
Draw strength from it.
Be empowered to continue on
no matter how many obstacles I face.
No matter how many difficulties and problems assail me.
No matter how many failures I must endure.

"One sows, another reaps" tells me there is no failure.
Just temporary setbacks.
That there is always possibility.

I am a branch and you,
Jesus dwelling within me,
are always supplying me with more life-giving sap
than I will ever use.
Your strength is my power.

Jesus, my indwelling friend,
I look at a crucifix.
For those without faith, the final failure.
For those with faith coursing through
their every spiritual vein,
the ultimate success.

You, Jesus, are the quintessential Sower.
You never stopped because some soils
did not receive the seeds of your revelation.
Yet, I take consolation from your complaints
about your closest friends,
"Oh, you of little faith.
How long will I put up with you?"

Your cross, indwelling friend, tells me that my failures
are treasures hidden in the field of my priestly endeavors.
And in my priestly ministry, from time to time,
I will stumble upon one or another treasure
encrusted with the disfiguring dirt of failure.

Stumbling is the metaphor for my ministry of seed-sower.
I stumble over ground
filled with growth-defying rocks
or soil wrapped in life-choking weeds.

I stumble along but all the while you are saying to me,
"Come, follow me."

If I start looking for the treasures,
I will become involved in the miserly desire for immediate results.
And all the surprises, you, my indwelling Lover, have in store for me
to delight me when I am feeling defeated in my priestly work,
will be lost to me.

What a consoling statement: "One sows, another reaps."
Jesus, identified with me, I feel so consoled
because you understand my poor human heart with infinite wisdom.
You continually implant possibilities in my failures
like a farmer scattering seeds with eternal abandon.

Did you not weep over Jerusalem?
"Jerusalem, Jerusalem, you who kill the prophets
and stone those sent to you,
how many times I yearned to gather your children together,
as a hen gathers her young under her wings,
but you were unwilling!"

How you tried. How you failed.

And yet the seeds you sowed have grown into a universal vine
with myriads of branches throughout the ages,
bearing the fruit of goodness, kindness,
forgiveness, compassion, love.

Even at those times
when futility seems to be the order of the day
and my soul is weary,
"One sows, another reaps" fills me with confidence.
It is the kind of confidence that gives me stamina to continue,
despite the lack of immediate results or out-and-out failures.

Eternal Trinity, Father, Son, and Spirit, dwelling within me,
I am filled with such exuberant joy.
You have called me to a most hallowed work as a priest.

Vulnerable as I am, you want me to warm hearts with your love,
to enlighten minds with your truth,
to affirm spirits with your hope.

Indwelling friend, Jesus, empower me to internalize your words
that you speak to me each day.
Help me to continue to sow the seeds of my faith-filled efforts
while not concerning myself with the harvest of immediate results.
Strengthen me to leave the harvesting of my seed-sowing to others
while I continue to gather the fruits from others' efforts.

3

Wandering Heart – Treasure Me

Loving Trinity, Father, Son, and Spirit,
dwelling within me,
closer to me than my own breath,
I continue to ponder the revelation of the mysterious
"One sows, another reaps."

The mystery of my seed-sowing ministry
is that I find what I'm *not* looking for.
That I treasure the surprises you allow me to discover
as I do the backbreaking work
of plowing and seeding.

There is more here than seeds and soil.

When I am doing the sowing, I must be authentically involved.
I can do some scattering, but I must be a careful planter too.

I never want to hear you, loving Word within me,
say to me what you said to the Pharisees and scribes, quoting Isaiah:
"This people honors me with their lips,
but their hearts are far from me."

Even less do I want to hear the last part of that prophecy:
"...teaching as doctrine, were human precepts."

How often do I preach your story, Jesus within me?
Offering insights that have grown out of the fertile soil
of my contemplative imagination?
Insights that challenge and encourage those seated before me
with all their various hungers?

How often do I preach my own fearful, severe moralism?
Or my own comfortable prejudices?

I may pound away at the need for chastity
and the horrors of sophisticated pornography in advertising.
But how often do I lift up my heart
and offer insights into your promise
that where our treasure is there will be our hearts?
How often do I challenge the people I serve
to discover what is their true treasure?

And, indwelling Trinity, Father, Son, and Spirit,
what about my own hunger?
Do I feel an ache in my heart
for the food your living words offer me?
How often do I truly meditate on doctrines
that emanate from your words addressed personally to me?

Or is the only time I make contact with your dynamic revelation
when I am trying to prepare a homily?
Even then do I first allow your word to challenge me
before I make it challenge the good people seated in front of me?

Not all the problems in my seed-sowing ministry
are due to the rejecting soil of people's hearts.

I, present within you dwelling within me, blessed, all-giving Trinity,
must check the quality of my own soil.
I must be open to the possibility that my soil
may be the source of problems in my priestly ministry.

I must be willing to admit that if mine is a sad heart
crinkled with discouragement and disappointments,
it might be due to my honoring you with frivolous lip service.

All-holy Trinity within me, how easy it is,
because of routine or familiarity,
for me to slip into honoring only with my lips
while my heart is on other treasures.

When I celebrate the Eucharist, for instance,
is my faith-conscious heart pounding fervently on my tongue?
Vibrating on my lips?
Infused into each word I have pronounced so many times,
over and over in the eucharistic prayer?

Is the eucharistic prayer I offer one of heartfelt love?
Or just another duty I must fulfill?

Certainly here in your indwelling presence,
I cannot give you lip service.
Not if I am honestly aware of your being within me
and I within you in the intimate precincts of my heart,
where I discover the fibers of honest self-understanding
and weave them into the seamless garment
of authentic communication with you.

Here within your indwelling presence of gracious gifting,
if I really and truly believe you are within me,
my heart cannot be far from you.

Here my heart dwells within your indwelling presence,
my lips kiss your living word,
and I am energized to go forth and sow the seed of your love,
no matter who reaps the harvest.

4

Enlightening Blind Man – Insight Me

Indwelling Trinity, living within me,
closer to me than my own soul,
I, your priest, want to be filled
with wonder and amazement
at the intimacy you desire to have with
me and with all those I serve.

I'm afraid that when it comes
to this most magnificent mystery of our mutual indwelling,
I am like the blind man of Bethsaida.

Like him who saw people looking like trees,
I look at the mystery of the Divine Indwelling
and see only an ancient doctrine
that doesn't seem to have much of an impact on my life
and therefore remains, if articulated at all,
a vague, abstract statement.

Often in my interactions with those
you ask me to serve as their priest,
your dwelling within me and within all of us
just isn't the fundamental fact,
the conscious dynamic of my relationships.

Unlike the blind man of Bethsaida,
I won't even wait for the second sweep of your majestic power
which will clarify my sight thoroughly
so that I can see this mystery of your indwelling "distinctly."

It boggles my mind, Jesus within me,
that after all my training for the priesthood
and the short or long years of being a priest,
I can still suffer your lashing indictment
that I have eyes but do not see.

The seeing you want from me
is a form of consciousness.
To "see" you dwelling within me,
within my priestly ministry,
within the people I work for and with
each day of my priesthood,
I must be fluidly conscious of the fact that you said
you and your Father would come and make your home
within me
and within my people.

I realize, indwelling God, that this consciousness, this "seeing,"
is not the immediate gratification of my desire
for greater holiness as a priest
but the awakening of my hope to enter more fully
into the process of becoming a saint
—no matter how skeptical I might be
about such a cloud-covered ideal.

I realize further that I must let go of the pattern
of the kind of consciousness that sustains
defeatist, negative thinking
about your luring me into a greater, deeper, more authentic,
more broadly sharing holiness.

If holiness was not a possibility,
my heart would not achingly crave it.

The story of the blind man of Bethsaida,
gaining his sight in two stages,
reveals to me that the more conscious I become
the more I realize how unconscious I have been.

Here I am, a priest.
Yet I must ask and honestly answer this question:
How conscious have I been of God's dwelling within me?
And this stimulates a corollary question:
How often have I preached on the Divine Indwelling
or even mentioned it?
For instance,
when introducing the Prayer of the Faithful,
how often do I pray,
"Let us offer our petitions to God, our *loving* God,
who lives intimately within us"?

I pray, indwelling Trinity,
that as with the blind man so with me:
help me to see clearly, distinctly.
Help me to be prophetically, mystically conscious
of the intimate presence of your loving indwelling within me.

This consciousness must look farther into our tradition
and see the connection with John's words in his first letter:
"God is love."

I pause here, indwelling Word, Jesus my friend,
and settle into that brief but all-encompassing insight,
the essence of my relationship with you
and with all the people I try to serve.
God is love.

How often have I read it? Heard it? Preached it?
Yet each time it makes an overture,
I am stunned into a kind of mystical realization.
You are love.
Your love prompts you to make your home within me
together with your Father and your Spirit.

You, Love itself,
infinite, boundless, reckless Love itself,
dwell within me and in all your people.
Since "God is love," then love is God.

This is the bond I must live with the people
you have called me to give my life to.
When I say, "I love my people," I am saying,
"God, who is indwelling Love itself,
within me and within others,
is my intimate bond with my people."

There can be no love without you, intimate Indweller.
There can be no authentic experience of you, indwelling God,
without love.

5

Gradual Visionary – Patience Me

Lord, infinite Creator of the universe,
dwelling in the depths of my being,
enlightening and challenging me, your priest,
I continue to ponder the blind man of Bethsaida.

Specifically, I am intrigued with the trees as a symbol.

Why did your inspired writer include the detail,
"I see people looking like trees and walking"?

First he sees people who look like trees.
In the second round of the healing he sees clearly and distinctly.

My entering into a sharper seeing consciousness
is not a quick, once-and-done event.
Rather, it is a slow process,
and I ask you, my indwelling Lover,
to give me the patience I need.

Help me not to look back and chastise myself
for all the times I have not been conscious
of you dwelling within me,
all the times I failed to accept
or have deliberately ignored your challenges.
This, I know, is wasted energy.

When I finally begin to take my spiritual growth seriously,
I tend to be a much more demanding taskmaster than you are.

I think of the six days of creation and try to realize
that slowness is not laziness,
that pondering is not procrastination,
that opportunities not taken can still be challenges to be met.

It takes time to develop my spiritual consciousness — slow time.
I need to ponder, think, review, compare, connect,
look within and without, absorb, internalize, enflesh.
This doesn't happen in the stroke of the hour.

The process of growing consciousness
waits for my entrance into it.
You, indwelling Lover, show me through the symbol of trees
that my entrance into a deeper, keener consciousness
of my relationship with you
depends on where I am on my road to Emmaus
— at the beginning of the journey or at an intermediate stage
or there in the inn of revelation.

But it is a painstaking journey to various levels of enlightenment,
not a flashy Olympic race to the gold of instant intuition.

At first, like the blind man, I may see with a vague consciousness.
But I know from this symbol of your revelation, indwelling friend,
that there will come a time when, with your power,
I will see with a clear and distinct consciousness at least for a time,
at least at certain turning points in my priestly ministry.

Unlike the blind man in the gospel story,
mine is a cycle where my seeing will go
from vague to clear and from clear to vague consciousness
all through my priestly pilgrimage here in this life.

I mustn't waste good energy fighting to break out of this cycle.
With patient trust in you, my all-powerful Indweller,
I go with it until all is light
and my seeing is always "clear and distinct."
You, my indwelling Guide, will win out
for you are "the Light of the world"
and you are forever transforming me into your light
so that I can be a light in my part of the world.

I ask again for patience, especially patience with myself.
You who are Eternity itself are dwelling within me.
You are the source of all my patience.
Help me to use the power of patience
you are always extending me.

The symbol of "people looking like trees and walking"
brings me out of myself to my relating
with those you have sent me to serve in my priestly ministry.

This image, indwelling Trinity, challenges me to examine honestly
how I encounter, relate to, and deal with the people
I have been ordained to nourish with my faith consciousness.

I may not treat people like things (trees), but I must ask myself,
as the routine of my daily ministry
slips into the measured regularity of the hands of a clock,
if I tend to treat people as "cases" or as "problems" to be solved,
or even as "annoyances" disrupting my plans for the day.

Am I aware that each person who walks into my life
for whatever reason
is a bearer of your revelation to me?
That if I am patiently involved in my process
of becoming more spiritually conscious,
this person can be a catalyst to my further growth in consciousness?

Whether a withered fig tree or a hospitable mustard tree,
whether weed or wheat,
each person has something to tell me about you,
my loving Indweller,
provided I am open to what each person is offering me.
Provided that I am convinced that I can learn from anyone,
from everyone.
Provided that I never think of my priestly vestments
as robes of all-knowing wisdom.

Am I conscious that you, indwelling Lover, living within me
are also living within this concrete person
standing or seated in front of me
or just gliding past me?

Help me, loving Indweller, never to become
so programmed or habituated in my priestly ministry
that I stop treating each person as sacred, as priceless.

Help me to see that each person
is "walking" in and out of my priestly life.
Sometimes people walk in to enhance and enrich my life as a priest.
Sometimes people walk away from me
indicating the need I have
to continue to enliven my consciousness of your indwelling
and your ideals and challenges for me,
to grow and become all you want me to be
so that I may walk steadfastly and courageously in your footsteps,
you whose ministerial priesthood I share.

I thank you for all the gifts of people you give me.
Help me to treasure them and never walk past them
unconscious of the ditch of suffering they may be trapped in.

6

Other Lost Sheep – Zeal Me

Jesus, my friend, dwelling within me,
closer to me than I am to myself,
I thank you for the gift of my ministerial priesthood.
You have called me to share
in your work of shepherding.

But often I find myself lingering with the ninety-nine
instead of seeking out the one who is lost.

It isn't that I am not interested in finding someone
who needs to be found and brought back.
Rather it's that I am so preoccupied
with the business of caring for those who are here
that I don't seem to have the time or energy
to pursue the one who has drifted away.

I ask you, Jesus, my friend,
living within me,
to increase my zeal.
May my zeal burn in my heart like a bonfire,
and spread throughout my life like a brush fire.

Help me never to look upon my ministry of shepherding
as mere duty.

Fill me with passion
so that I will approach all those
you have entrusted to my care
with enthusiastic zeal,
whether they are here within the sheepfold
or have wandered off
to what they think are greener pastures.

Sometimes I tend to get discouraged
by the number of those who are no longer active
in our community of faith.

I know from past experiences
that negative fantasies or memories can cause me
anxiety and worry,
fear and depression,
and a defensive attitude.
I know that the more I dwell
in these kinds of fantasies or memories
the worse they get.

Yet I want to be the kind of shepherd
who has a zeal that is rapturous interest and excitement,
ardent eagerness, enthusiasm, passion, and liveliness.

I recognize that I choose the thoughts I think.
Therefore, in my negative moods,
I need to change my thinking.
I ask you for the strength to think positive thoughts
about ministering to those who have faded
from the scene of communal faith-living.

I dwell within the image of your going out of your way
to reach out to the Canaanite woman
whose daughter was tormented by a demon.

I want to draw strength from your interaction with this woman
so that when I am called upon to inconvenience myself
to contact someone who has given up
on worshiping with our faith community,
I will do so.

Help me, indwelling friend,
to make your words my habitual attitude:
"I have other sheep who do not belong to this fold.
These also I must lead, and they will hear my voice,
and there will be one flock, one shepherd."

7

Ever-Chastening Commitment – Solitude Me

Father, Son, and Spirit,
dwelling within me,
there are times in my priestly ministry
when I feel painfully, exasperatingly alone.
I shudder at the prospect that this shabby loneliness
might envelop me for a much longer time than I can ever bear.

I try to listen to my heart,
not for words of wisdom or direction
but for my heart's silences and stillness.
But I hear nothing.
I try to enter into the midnight lurking
of my repressed emotions
but with no success.

I think of the commitment I made at my ordination.
But this thought doesn't seem to bring me much consolation.

Commitment seems to be such a drudge-word.
For me at least, it conjures up the picture
of crawling across the desert floor of life
or of being joylessly tied down
when every pulse of my heart wants to soar in free-spirit freedom
or even in giddy risk.

I'd rather substitute the word "passion"
for the word "commitment."
Passion carries within it the feel of
initiative, exuberance, creativity,
hope, fancifulness, enjoyment,
pursuit, wonder, awe,
energy, enthusiasm, self-motivation,
renewal, possibility, fulfillment,
and emancipation from manufactured restrictions.

Loving Trinity within me,
you enable me to visit the attic of my memory
where mementos of an earlier passion
regenerate my zeal.
Here I find a new feeling:
that my sluggish loneliness is not icy isolation.

Rather it is a reinvigorating preparation
for extending myself more fervently to others,
even if this means that at times all I have to offer
is my emptiness as my gift.
And in return, I am able to receive from others
whatever they offer to fill my emptiness,
to sweeten my feeling of loneliness.

I ponder a thought from Father John Powell:
"For those who accept themselves,
being alone is peaceful solitude;
for those who don't,
solitude is painful loneliness."

My feeling of loneliness is a school
where I can take a refresher course in self-acceptance.
Through my loneliness I relearn that self-acceptance is essential
if I am ever going to experience the sweetness of serenity.

Father, Son, and Spirit, so lovingly close to me,
help me to use the times of loneliness, which ambush me,
in a positive, growth-producing way.
Help me to use my feelings of loneliness
to reach out and extend a healing touch
to those who are helplessly submerged in their loneliness.

But above all, help me to use my loneliness
as an opportunity to come more consciously to you within me.
Help me to be keenly aware
that no matter how empty I may feel,
you are filling me with yourself,
my loving, indwelling God.

8

Tassel-Touching Trembler – Courage Me

Eternal, triune God, Father, Son, and Spirit,
living with infinite intimacy within me,
there are times in my spiritual life
when I feel like the parched bottom of a dried-up lake.
In these times,
I wonder how I will be able to feel happy in my priestly work,
spread joy among my people,
or preach your message with enthusiasm and visible conviction.

Sometimes I feel emotionally depleted, and I'm not sure why.
Perhaps it's because I am making so little headway
in my own spiritual development
or because I am unable to stoke the fires of zeal in others
or because my best laid plans find no support, only criticism.
Whatever the reason, I feel devitalized.

Despite this spiritual aridity,
I know that you are dwelling profusely within me,
even though I can feel nothing.
I know that your indwelling does not depend on my feelings
but is your gracious gift.
In fact, through this spiritual aridity you are telling me to seek you
who are the God of consolations, not the consolations of God.

I am aware of these faith facts
but that does not alleviate my feelings of desolation.
Still I believe that you are constantly offering me
all the strength I need to fulfill my priestly duties
with joyous zeal and loving compassion.

Even as I pray to you within me,
my spiritual and physical energy seems to have hemorrhaged.
I identify with the woman suffering hemorrhages for twelve years
who comes up behind you, Jesus,
and touches the tassel on your cloak.
With her I say, "If only I can touch his cloak, I shall be cured."

Paradoxically, you may be curing
the external hemorrhaging of my energy
with my interior dryness.

I also need to be cured of my craving
for ego-satisfying or ego-enhancing rewards
for the priestly service you have called me to.

This woman reminds me once again that I am unique.
When she touches the tassel of your cloak,
it is as if time stands still.

She is no longer lost in the crowd.
She is now the focus of your total attention.
There is no one in the world but this woman
and nothing but her need.
So too with me.

The captivating aspect in this story is that for you,
Jesus, my indwelling friend,
no one is ever lost in the crowd.
I think of what the poet W. B. Yeats wrote
in one of his moments of mystical beauty:

"The love of God is infinite for every human soul
because every human soul is unique....
God gives all of himself to each individual person."

Whether I am experiencing consolations or not,
you, indwelling God,
are giving yourself to me totally, absolutely, unconditionally.
You are always here within me!
Your presence within me is unique to me.
This I believe.

Jesus within me,
I take into my heart your reassurance to this woman:
"Courage, daughter."
I need courage to recognize that my strength
comes not only from your consolations,
but even more so from the state of my spiritual dryness.
I need courage to maintain my belief
that it is you who can grow the most beautiful flowers
in the parched soil of my heart
and cast light into the dark night of my soul.

It strikes me that the wonderfully revealing truth
in this episode of your earthly life
is that unlike the woman with the hemorrhages,
I do not have to sneak up behind you
but that I have a constant entrée into your presence
and that of your Father and Spirit within me.

Here in your presence
I need the courage to appear before you,
stripped of all my desires to be comforted.
Courage to be ready
and eager to accept all the challenges you give me,
especially the challenge to endure spiritual aridity.

Your healing of this woman symbolizes for me
that you are unconditionally available to me,
that your power is always going out from you
into my life and priestly ministry as a healing flow of affirmation.

Eternally loving Trinity within me, another thought comes to me.
You are challenging me to do more than endure my spiritual aridity.
Help me to use it to become
less self-centered in my spiritual development
and in the work of my priestly ministry.

Through my spiritual dryness
I am able to sharpen my realization that warm, fuzzy feelings
can merely be the soft underbelly of sentimentality,
not the sturdy rock of faith.

My spiritual aridity reminds me, indwelling friend,
that you became human so that you could permeate and sanctify
my every thought, tear, smile, hope,
feeling or lack of feeling, and undertaking
and that the meaning of my life, of my priesthood, of my spirituality
is more often arrived at by dark gropings
than by bright and light fanciful feelings.

When all my feelings
of exuberance, enthusiasm, joy, delight, elation are dried up,
help me to cling to the faith fact
that you are always dwelling within me.
That my dwelling within you is not rooted in my feelings
but in the courageous faith you have given me.

9

Blessed Peacemakers – Disturb Me

Jesus, my indwelling friend, a priest told me
that one morning, at the Sign of Peace,
a woman took his hand into hers and whispered,
"May the peace of Christ disturb you."

The priest went on to say,
"I paused momentarily,
trying to assimilate this strange greeting,
and then moved on.
The woman left Mass immediately after the blessing.
For the rest of the day, her greeting haunted me
like the memory of the colors of a winter's sunset
which I couldn't name.

"I wondered: Could her greeting mean something like
when people get all their rights,
they will still complain about all their wrongs?
No, that wasn't quite it.

"Then it dawned on me that the peace of Christ,
like no other kind of peace,
disturbs my complacency, my self-satisfaction,
my feeling that I have *arrived,*" the priest concluded.

The ideal of peacemaking is always a challenge, isn't it, Jesus?
With all the conflicts,
whether interpersonal or international,
in the world,
with nations being convinced that peace can be maintained
by having the best implements of war,
with familial abuse, both physical and psychological,
how can I ever rest?

Your peace, Jesus my indwelling friend, is always stretching me
even to the point of anguish
to bring more and greater peace into the lives of those I am serving
and the people all around me.

I realize that part of my priestly ministry is to make certain
that the various colors of differing attitudes and stances
must not be used as war paint
but must be harmonized into a gorgeous rainbow.
I can't do this if I keep all disunity and feuds locked away
in an impenetrable strong box.

Right here in my parish there are so many splinter groups.
It's one thing for my people to have varying perceptions
of how to practice their religion.
But it's altogether something else
when they turn these perceptions into battlefields,
when they unleash the weapons
of harsh condemnations and violent accusations
which prevent them from truly living their faith
while sanctimoniously practicing their version of religion.

I begin to realize that you, Jesus, who are my interior Peace,
are disrupting my desire to escape from the problems of peace,
from the efforts required to bring about harmony among my people
and within the community at large.

As long as there is friction or discord of any kind,
I cannot rest in your peace, Jesus.
Rather I must take the peace you give me
and allow it to disturb my restfulness
so that I can genuinely share that peace with all others.

The peace you give me is not a refuge
where I can bask in my apathy.
Rather your peace is a disturbance,
challenging me to be a peacemaker.

Jesus, my indwelling friend,
I need courage to confront the built-in tension
between peacemakers and power-mongers,
whether these power-mongers are members of my parish
or members of the corporate complex.

As a peacemaker,
I must preach peace and demonstrate for peace
when my state government advocates and pursues the death penalty.
I must be a peacemaker when my national government
sends so-called peacekeeping forces into another country
where innocent people and children become victims
of nothing less than warfare.

I must be a peacemaker
when the Supreme Court justices legalize abortion
by protesting a decision that promulgates the falsehood
that what has been made legal is moral.

I am convinced, Jesus, my indwelling friend, that in our culture
where civil religion begs God to bless its bombs
and preserve its wealth,
there is little room for true religion
which calls peacemakers and the poor "blessed."

I believe that to be an authentic peacemaker,
I must be countercultural.
I must assess our culture's agenda and vested interests
within the framework of my faith, in the light of the gospel values.
And I must do all I can
to help the people I am serving to do the same.

To be a true peacemaker, I must convince my people
that our culture cannot impose on us its values and priorities
that contradict the values and priorities of gospel faith.

This, Trinity within me, is no easy task.
It's a lot easier to just drift along,
hoping that my people can keep their balance
with one foot in the world of faith
and another in the world of our culture's values,
which are opposed to our fundamental beliefs as followers of Jesus.

I ask you, Jesus, my indwelling friend, to help me always
to let your peace disturb my tendency to compromise, to cut corners,
to adapt to a civil religion that puts more emphasis
on saluting the flag than on living your teachings.

Help me, with my words and in my actions,
to preach peace fearlessly and courageously.
Let the peace you infuse into me be a bulwark against those
who criticize me for being unpatriotic or, worse, a traitor
because I question the intentions of our governmental leaders.

Help me to use my priestly ministry to create a peaceful world
where each person is valued like a pearl of priceless worth,
where all persons are loved and accepted for who they are,
where every person is honored and served
because they are created in the image and likeness of you.

10

Divining Desert – Distill Me

Jesus, my indwelling friend, it was in a desert place
where the tempter slithered in and around his traps
like one slipping stones into a baker's oven.

I ponder how the tempter tried to trick you,
the Jordan pilgrim,
drenched as you had been in divine words of approval
— "I find my pleasure in him" —
and dried in the flutter of the dove's descent.

As I ponder this event in your earthly life,
I am filled with courage by your refusal
to succumb to temptations of ego power.
What a lesson for me in my priestly ministry
where it is so easy for me
to use the power of my priesthood tyrannically
in order to make people walk the straight and narrow
instead of using that power as gentle persuasion.

Jesus, my indwelling friend,
it was in a desert place
where you the carpenter from Nazareth
nailed your audience's attention
by proclaiming the promise of living bread.

You watched your followers,
many of whom had come to you to be touched and cured,
walk away, deserting you
because your sayings were just too hard.

Even to this day
as I try to fulfill my priestly obligations,
indwelling friend,
your sayings are hard.
You challenge me to turn the other cheek
when someone I have tried to help turns on me
and slaps me with lashing ingratitude
or a false accusation or a public denunciation.
You expect me to walk an extra mile with someone
who pesters me beyond endurance
or with someone who whines or bores me
until I'm totally stressed out.
Yet I pray over your words,
"Without me you can do nothing,"
and conclude that with you within me
with your infinite power,
I can persevere.
In the divine paradox,
your hard sayings become for me tender invitations.

Jesus, my indwelling friend,
in that desert place of promised flesh to eat,
your religious leaders
who set their own traps
of Caesar's coin and Sabbath rules,
joined in the chorus of questioning
how you could break your flesh into food
and defamed your miraculous promise
as the work of Beelzebul, the prince of devils.

How your heart must have ached.
Yet you continued on. You never backed down.
You, the Word, always kept your word.
I can only respond by being steadfast in proclaiming your word
even when those with authority, those with power
belittle me because I disturb their complacency.

So it was that you, my indwelling friend,
went into desert places to search the will of him who sent you.
There, with your Father and Spirit,
you confront the question of your power:
"Who touched me?"
There you ponder the living good news
of cured lepers and shrieking exorcisms,
of the blind staring in wonder
at cripples dancing to the songs of the mute.

Each day, as I begin anew my priestly mission,
I must consult your will, indwelling Father.
Fundamentally I know that your will for me
is that I continue to grow and develop
through my priestly interactions with the people I serve.
Most of the time it is difficult for me
to discern the specifics of your will
in given, concrete situations,
but as long as I strive to be selfless and generous,
reasonably available and calmly empathetic,
I am fulfilling your will,
your daily call to become all you want me to be.

At the end of each day, I try to run the tape of that day
to discover the wonders you work through me:
people scarred by disputes with loved ones, healed;
people plagued by a demon of stubbornness or vindictiveness
or egotism or obnoxiousness, exorcised;

people crippled by betrayal or rash judgments
or detraction or sorrow, able to stand again on their own two feet;
people silenced by fear or indifference or boredom,
speaking out on behalf of justice and peace.

And I feel renewed, energized, rededicated
thanks to your power flowing like a fountain within me,
my indwelling Strength.

I ask you, eternal Trinity within me,
to guide me so that I will not use my desert places
as an escape from the turmoil of people's expectations of me.
Expectations too urgent for me to flee.
Expectations pressing like incurable flesh
against my weakened human power.

Jesus, you who are the Light shining within and through me,
help me to enter into the dry irony of my desert places
where the sands of escape shift quickly
into the sandstorms of confrontation with my sinful barrenness,
with the tempter's lure into apathy,
with false promises that strain my zeal.
Jesus within me, you who are the Way,
help me to emerge from my desert places
cleansed, encouraged, and revitalized.

11

Habitual Resurrection – Peace Me

Jesus, my indwelling friend,
I ponder your Resurrection.

It strikes me that your enemies had rolled the stone of rejection
in front of your teachings, your stories,
your call for self-sacrificing discipleship
long before they rolled the stone of burial in front of your tomb.

In their whitewashed plottings, they had appealed to civil religion:
"Is it lawful to pay the census tax to Caesar or not?"
"It is expedient that one man die rather than a whole nation perish."

Your followers, Jesus within me, like scattered sheep,
withdrew from the tomb, hurrying off,
one step beyond the waters parted by blood,
a side issue to your dying gasp that quaked like Spirit.

They went off to search for words once written in sand
and ponder the grain of wheat
before it could rise into a white harvest.

Your disciples buried themselves in their own tomb
—a room bolted against the echoes of mocking insolence
still piercing their unnerved memories.
"He saved others, himself he cannot save."

They stayed there in that room
until they heard their name anew: "Peace."

How much I,
who profess belief in your Resurrection,
am like them.
How I board myself up against the onslaughts of injustice,
hoping it will somehow just go away.
Here I am a leader of my people, but I am not worth my salt
if my actions are guided by fear of criticism or of losing support.

Yet I believe your resurrection power is within me,
always available to me if I am willing to use it.

Your resurrection story continues in my story today.
The grain of wheat still dies to bear much fruit.

In my own time, a bullet is fired as smooth as silence.
A wound splits a life open like a bag of grain.
Blood pours out over the altar of sacrifice.
A bishop named Romero in El Salvador falls to the ground and dies.
And he is now being harvested as "Peace."

Your resurrection story is being retold
each time the barriers of bigotry, aloofness, oppression,
exploitation, hatred, and manipulation
are removed like a stone rolled away from a tomb.

Your resurrection story is being retold
each time I, your priest, realize that death to my false self
means resurrection to my real self.
That my every failure is a call to rise again.

Your resurrection story is being retold
each time I, in my priestly ministry, use your resurrection power
to cause resurrections in the people I am serving.

Just as you rose out of death into new life,
empower me to help others
to rise out of the death of depression or anxiety or hopelessness
into the new life of optimism and trust and joy.

Your resurrection story is being retold
each time I recognize in broken bread and shared cup
each person's right to a fair share of this world's resources.
Each time I labor in my plot of the vineyard
until all on earth are Easter people.

Jesus, my indwelling Lover, increase my faith consciousness
so that I will habitually cause resurrections in my people.
Fill me with the exuberant joy of your rebirth
so that I can bring comfort and hope
into the lives of those I am serving.
Challenge me through them
to leave behind the tomb of my dying to self
and rise to the new life you are always offering me.

12

Oceans of Faith – Dream Me

Eternal Trinity, Father, Son, and Spirit, I remember a time when I sat pondering the ocean, extending far out to an edge where eye could see no more than sky and ocean touching.

I thought of our early ancestors:
some walked along the ocean.
But their lives were inland.
Others stopped and fleetingly wondered
about the extent of the ocean, shrugged and moved on.
Still others looked out at the vast expanse
and longed to know what was beyond
but walked away, doing nothing.
Finally there were those who pined to know
where the ocean extended to.
They built ships and set sail to explore.

I thought this was an interesting analogy
for faith as opposed to religion.
Some never notice the breadth and depth of faith.
Others sometimes think about it
but move along with no more thought.
Still others have an inkling
that there has to be much more to faith than what they see.
They wonder but do nothing.

Finally there are those who launch out into the deep
and explore the vastness of their faith.

I thought too of how today
we can fly over this mystery called ocean in a few hours,
totally oblivious of its existence.
The analogy: how we can become so preoccupied
with our own interests and distractions
that we don't even notice our faith in our pilgrimage.

I thought also of you, the Creator God,
and of you, the Cosmic Christ
—the unfathomable depth, the vastness of it all!

Lord, dwelling within me,
I look upon my dreams fading gray in the blue of my hope.
Dashed they are and drifting, drifting down until I barely see them.
Boyhood dreams of the difference I would make,
and now the purpose of my life is just clinging to the dream,
no longer worrying whether or not it will come true.
Indwelling friend,
just let me hang on to the dream
that no matter what else is said of me,
the stone may read,
Here lie the bones of a dreamer,
but his dream still haunts our hearts.

13

Be-Perfected Calling – Sensitize Me

It can happen to me, indwelling Trinity,
after a piddling confrontation.
I feel staggeringly foolish
or, more accurately, incoherently embarrassed.

With the sudden clarity of soul-piercing honesty,
I recognize and admit to myself
(I don't have the courage to admit it to anyone else
except to you within me)
that I just lost it.
My words went from patient gentility to stormy harshness.

In the face of the other person's criticism,
I became defensive and then defiant.
I blundered into a best-defense-is-a-good-offense stance.

I want so much to appear noble,
able to transcend, like an eagle in flight,
the pettiness of interpersonal clashes.
Yet here I was allowing myself to plummet into a crude repartee.

Now I have to begin all over
to get back to the root principle of the kind of person I want to be:
Christ-like.

How often in my priesthood have I had to do this?
How many times have I failed
to live up to the ideal I should be living as your priest?

There are times when I feel discouragement
bordering on the sluggish crossfire of despondency
not because I have faults
(I'm rational enough to know I am imperfect)
but because I so often advertise my faults.

How often have I preached
patient listening, understanding empathy?
This person has heard my homilies.
What must he think? Actions speak louder than words?
Is he thinking that I talk the talk but don't walk the walk?

Whatever he is thinking about me, I know how I feel.
I feel immobilized in the straightjacket of humiliation.

Here in my praying,
my communicating with you within me,
I think of Peter.

Despite his humiliating experience of denying you,
he was able to insist, "You know that I love you."
And you, Jesus, my indwelling friend,
who rose out of death into new life,
empowered Peter to rise out of his mangling despondency
into the new life of rhapsodic hopefulness.

I ask you to empower me
to rise out of my anger with my failure
into the new life of honest self-examination
so that I can continue in my efforts of self-renewal.
On the practical level,
I know I must go to that person and apologize.

Even more, I must thank him for his critique
and tell him that I will try to profit from what he said.

In this way, I will move from humiliation to humility.
I will be able to live what I say I believe, namely,
that I am human therefore limited therefore imperfect
but, thanks to your grace,
I wholeheartedly believe that I am also perfectible.

Jesus, my indwelling friend,
quiet the tempestuous impulses of my heart.
Convert my heart into a place of blissful peace for others,
especially those who launch militant diatribes at me.

Let me experience your Resurrection power
as a surge of my hope and vitality.
Help me to remember the pain of my faults and failures
so that I will be ever more sensitive
to the weaknesses of others.

14

Bushel-Basketed Lamp – Bonfire Me

Eternal Father within me,
you are the Creator of the very first glimmer of light.
"Let there be light!"
Jesus, my indwelling friend, you said,
"I am the Light."
There is a saying from the Christophers:
"It's better to light one candle than to curse the darkness."

I've heard this so often that I recite it
without plumbing the depths of its wisdom.
Yet now I am meditating on this adage
in the context of the many times
when I felt so helpless in a world
of brazen cruelty,
haughty defiance,
boorish selfishness,
grudgebearing hard-heartedness,
random violence.

In my priestly ministry, there have also been times
when I wanted to do something to heal this world,
but since powerful governments can't do much,
I have found myself asking, "What can I do?"

Yet instead of giving in to my feeling of helplessness,
I dwell on the image of that one candle.
It isn't much
given the enveloping, pervasive darkness of our world,
but it is light.

I am well aware that if I do give in to a feeling of helplessness,
I am shoving the lamp of my priestly commitment
under a bushel basket.
The purpose of my lamp is to make things clear in the darkness,
to light the way for others to find you living within them.

Still I stop to think for a moment.
Instead of asking, "What can I do?"
I imagine millions upon millions of people
each one lighting one candle.
What becomes of that thick, deep darkness?
Isn't it dispelled?

Now I think of where I can light my one candle.
For whom?
How will I light it?
I can always light the candle of a kind word
or of a courteous gesture.
It may be nothing great
except that greatness resides
in the small actions of everyday living.

Or perhaps I could light my one candle of confrontation
with someone who is addicted,
maybe to alcohol or obnoxiousness or paranoia.

I realize that lighting my candle requires daring and risk.
But without risk I will continue doing
what I've always been doing,
and I will be what I've always been.

So I will light my candle.
And for a while the darkness will be dissipated.
The darkness may come back,
and, if it does, I'll just have to light yet another candle.

I know that I must believe with all the strength of my faith
that love lights far more fires than hatred can ever extinguish.

Jesus, my indwelling friend, you also said,
"You are the light."
What a challenge!
The candle I light is not out there but inside me.
And then there is an even deeper,
more exciting, more challenging insight:
I *am* your candle!

With your Pentecostal flame, indwelling Spirit,
light me, your candle.
I recall a prayer:
I am only a spark.
Make me a bonfire.

I ask you, Spirit within me,
to help me to enter into a fiery contemplation
ignited by the flames of passionate love.

Through your inspiration, indwelling Spirit, I am convinced
that it is in this passionate contemplation
that I will find the renewed stamina of my priestly ardor
so that I will not be crushed by feelings of helplessness.

You are not a God who rests complacently
in your omnipotence
up there on your eternal throne
while I struggle in a tormenting maze with no exit.

Rather I believe that your omnipotence means for me
and for the people I serve
that in every destructive situation,
you give me the inner power to overcome, to be victorious.

As I take up the duties of my ministry this day,
Trinity within me,
help me to keep alive in my consciousness
the indisputable fact that evil may at times triumph
but it never conquers.

I urgently want to be what you want me to be,
Jesus, my indwelling friend:
a light in the world.
I want to be a light that brightens my people's lives.
I want to be a light that brings warmth to people's hearts.
I want to be a light that kindles the fire of love
in people's relationships with one another.

Help me, Light of the world within me,
by blending your light with my light
until you and I are one light,
shining into all the people I come into contact with,
all the people I am privileged to serve.

15

Dual Masters – Counterculture Me

Jesus, my friend, dwelling within me, whose priesthood I share,
I have been pondering your statement,
"No one can serve two masters."

I believe that you are my master.
But my culture with the sorcery of subliminal propaganda
persistently tries to make itself my master.

I find that it is so easy to profess my faith in your values, Jesus,
while unconsciously submitting to the values of our culture,
which contradict yours.

I preach peace
in a world where countries decide to
drop bombs
on innocent, non-combative citizens.
And I find myself taking refuge
in comfortable expressions of religion.

I may not agree with the decisions of diplomats
but, at the same time, I do not publicly or officially
question their policies.
I do not make public or official demands for the truth
behind the rationalizations that governments offer.

Then in a moment of personal truth, I am forced to ask myself,
Am I serving two masters
by giving in to respectable compromises?

I listen to global leaders' high-pressure promises
about a better, more secure, more prosperous world.
But I do not confront those leaders
about the obvious poverty, homelessness,
alienation, and dehumanization
of the helplessly marginalized.

Then in a moment of personal truth, I am forced to ask myself,
Am I serving two masters?

Jesus, my indwelling friend, I need to be more countercultural.
I need to put the force and prestige of my priestly ministry
into counteracting those values in our culture
which oppose and contradict the values of the gospel,
whether subtly or overtly.

Prayerfully, I need to assess our culture's agenda
within the framework of the faith I profess
and am supposed to be living.
But I must do more.
I must take the realistic criticisms of our culture
which result from that assessment into the public forum.
And I must do this even if it means that I will be attacked
for being unpatriotic or malicious or fanatical
or radical or reactionary or subversive.

I am convinced that this is certainly a pivotal way
of lighting that one candle.

At the same time I need to make certain that I am not a fanatic,
cloaking my crusade with the banner of moral superiority.

If I am to make any headway in being countercultural,
I must be persuasive rather than dictatorial,
reasonable rather than tyrannical.
I must choose the spoonful of honey
rather than the barrel of vinegar.

I know from experience that put-downs cause turn-offs.

Jesus, my indwelling friend,
as I meditate on being more countercultural,
I think back to your first disciples.

In the early church,
your disciples brought the Good News to Gentiles.
And in doing so, they went against their own culture
as well as against the pagan culture.

In a word, your first disciples were countercultural.

As a result they ran into the buzz saw of misunderstanding,
ridicule, persecution, and ultimately martyrdom.

You yourself experienced such ridicule, misunderstanding,
denouncements, persecution, and martyrdom.

I know that when I am trying to be fervent
in living my faith counterculturally,
there will be those who accuse me of being holier-than-thou.
Sadly these accusations may come
even from those I expect to support me.

Or when I try to work for justice and peace
like protesting capital punishment or abortion
I know I will be sneered at for being an unbridled zealot.
Or when I go out of my way to conserve the environment,
I know people will mock me as a tree-hugger.

Or when I am patient and forgiving,
for instance, with those who repeatedly take advantage of me,
I know my friends will warn me
that I'm making myself a doormat.

The early disciples, men and women,
had the courage to live and proclaim your teachings, Jesus.
Nothing has changed much since then.
I need courage today to live and proclaim your teachings
in a culture that ridicules the gospel values
or ignores them as irrelevant.

Help me, Jesus, my indwelling friend,
to avoid slipping into cozy compromises with our culture.
Help me to avoid privatizing my faith,
making my faith a matter of otherworldly concerns
without giving any consideration to the flesh-and-blood needs
of those who are needlessly suffering
here and now in this world.

You, Jesus, my indwelling friend,
are my only, my one, true master.
Empower me to believe this with such passion
that I will live my priesthood
in a total, absolute, countercultural way.

Part Two

SAINTLY INTERCESSIONS

16

Mary – Persevere Me

Mary, Mother of Jesus and my Mother,
I entrust my priesthood to your care.

Two images come to mind when I pray to you:
your holding Jesus, the babe of Bethlehem,
and your holding Jesus, the crucified.
The Incarnation and the Redemption.

I ask you to obtain for me, Mary, my Mother,
the incarnational grace of being transformed
more and more into Christ, your Son.
And I ask your intercession that my priestly ministry
will always be one of redeeming the people I serve
from whatever holds them back from becoming
all that the indwelling God wants them to be.

This is my vocation.
This is my work.
This is my life.

Help me to be like you, Mary, my Mother,
treasuring in my heart
all the wonderful gifts and blessings
that God has bestowed on me.

I want to habitually review
all that God is doing for me in my priestly ministry
so that I will approach my people
with a heart overflowing with joyous gratitude.

So often, Mother Mary,
I find myself concentrating on the things that go wrong,
on the hurts others inflict on me,
on the deprivations I may suffer,
in a word, on the negatives in my life.

I need to have a more positive outlook.
And I know you can help me.

I want to be able to look at the crucifix and see Easter.
I want to be able to always look around for the wine
when I find myself in the cellar of affliction.
I want to treat failure and rejection
as information about how I can do better.

I know from experience that I have a choice:
I can dwell on negative outcomes
or on positive projections.
Help me to choose the latter.

With a more positive attitude, Mary, my Mother,
I can approach the people I am serving with greater hope,
and this is certainly what they need.

When I stand at the pulpit on the weekend,
I need to realize that the people before me
have come from a week of hardships, difficulties,
disappointments, tensions, heartbreaks.
And they are looking to me to give them a reason
to go back into their daily lives and try again, to persevere.

Mary, my Mother, you persevered,
going from one quandary to another
during your Son's public ministry.
You know what people need
and you can help me to feed them
the solid food of the gospel
to nourish them in their perseverance.
Your life and your relationship with Jesus
can nurture positive experiences and outcomes in me
and in the people I serve.

Help me, Mother of joy and Mother of sorrow,
to bring reinforcement into people's lives
and to empathize with people's problems
even while I myself am looking
for understanding and support.

Help me, Mary, my Mother,
to kneel before the crib of Bethlehem
and stand beneath the cross of Calvary
all the days of my priesthood,
believing with all my heart that your Son,
now my risen Lord,
is always with me and within me,
strengthening me with his resurrection power
to persevere.

17

Joseph – Confidence Me

There is something almost humorous
about your situation, St. Joseph.
There you were living with two people
who had never experienced sin!
In lighter moments, I wonder to whom the finger was pointed
when something went wrong.

For example, when the twelve-year-old Jesus was lost,
were you held accountable because,
as head of the family we call holy,
you were Jesus' guardian?

Yet, in your scant biographical sketch in the gospel story,
you, St. Joseph, were the hero of the infancy narrative.
You were a man who listened to your dreams
and understood their deep and real meaning.
You were like your namesake, Joseph of Egypt,
who in interpreting the pharaoh's dreams saved God's chosen people.

You were the just man, St. Joseph, who decided to be merciful
about Mary's socially embarrassing situation of being pregnant.
Instead of exposing her to the Law,
you chose to dissolve your engagement quietly.

Then in a dream you were told
to take the pregnant Mary into your home as your wife.
You did so.
In dreams you were instructed
to take Mary and the baby Jesus to Egypt
and to return to your homeland,
which you did faithfully.
You always took your dreams seriously.

Often we are told that daydreaming
is a waste of precious time.
But aren't my daydreams often the source
of my visions for the future of my priestly ministry?
Don't my positive daydreams infuse daring into my plans
and reinforce my willingness to take risks?

My daydreams, St. Joseph, confront me with a choice:
I can look at what is and ask why
or I can dream about what could be and ask why not.

Even in difficult times,
I need to keep dreaming of what could be.
Horrible things do happen
and I can't always change them.
But because I keep dreaming, I will,
with your help, St. Joseph,
continue working to try to change them for the better.

Sadly there are those among the people I serve
who have no dreams, no visions;
they just try to get through the day.

Yet I learn from you, St. Joseph,
that the future belongs to those
who believe in the beauty of their dreams.
And I want to be numbered among them.

I truly believe that I can help put an end to despair
by dreaming great dreams which, if and when fulfilled,
will add to the grandeur of humankind.

I am also convinced, St. Joseph, that without dreams
it is very difficult for love to flourish
and without love there will be no dreams.

My daydreams tell me
that there is far more to my priestly ministry
than keeping the Commandments
or just doing what I am told.
My daydreams can be the wellspring
of my initiative to follow my conscience
even when those around me are seeking refuge
in the antigospel values of our culture.

St. Joseph, help me to believe
that I can make my dreams a reality.

My daydreams offer me novel possibilities
for my future personal development as a human being
and for a more generous interpersonal sharing
in my priestly ministry.

St. Joseph, help me also to be more intensely prayerful
as I'm sure your were in the midst of all your dilemmas.
It is my prayer that will keep my hope active
and will restore life to the dead bones of my dreams.

Help me, St. Joseph, to make my daydreams
the foundation of a creative priestly ministry.
A creativity that will empower me
to enter into the unknown
with trust and confidence just as you did.

18

John Vianney – Balance Me

St. John Vianney, dear Curé,
when I think of your indefatigable zeal, I feel embarrassed.
Today, I suppose, you'd be tagged a workaholic.

This opens up an interesting question for me as a priest:
What is the difference between Christian zeal
and psychological workaholism?

Today, St. John, we priests are being told by psychologists
that we need to make room in our lives for ourselves,
to take care of our needs,
to make certain that we don't overextend ourselves
lest we burn out.

There's even a saying.
When we are too available to others,
we won't be available to ourselves.

In fact, St. John,
there is a lot being written about burnout.

Then I meditate on your life.
You must have experienced some kind of burnout
since three times you tried to leave your parish
and become a Carthusian.

By a strange twist of irony, that makes me feel a little better.

But then you came back.
Back to what we would call today the "rat race."
Or was it, in fact, back to persevering zeal?

Sometimes I wonder,
especially after meditating on your life, St. John,
if there's just too much emphasis on taking care of ourselves,
if avoiding burnout is just an excuse
for not giving of ourselves more generously.

Like any good advice,
taken to an extreme, avoiding burnout can become a debility,
a negative influence on my priestly work.

As in all things, what I need is balance:
sufficient recreation to relax
and sufficient work to fulfill my priestly calling
to the service of those entrusted to me.

Someone said: Without passion there is no enthusiasm,
without enthusiasm there is no zeal,
without zeal there is only duty.

I know that when I make an idol out of my work, I'm in trouble.
When work is my god, workaholism will be my worship.

St. John, I know from meditating on your life
that your zeal was rooted in the gospel.
It is the gospel that must motivate me in my priestly endeavors.
Zeal without the gospel will deteriorate into workaholism.
Zeal without the gospel will be like a ship without a rudder.

St. John, I ask you to intercede for me
that I may balance needed relaxation
with zealous work on behalf of those I serve.

19

Philip Neri – Humorize Me

St. Philip Neri,
I am amused at your penchant for practical jokes.
I remember reading about how you told a man
to whom you were giving spiritual direction
to shave half his face and go around with only half a beard.

Perhaps he was a man of pretentious vanity
who was in need of greater humility.

I wonder if I told someone to do the same thing, St. Philip,
how long would that man keep me as a spiritual director?

Then there was the occasion, St. Philip,
when you told a gossipy woman
to throw a bag of feathers into the wind
and then go and collect each feather.
When she protested,
you told her words of gossip were like those feathers,
once loosed, impossible to take back.
This has become a commonplace in our preaching
about the evil of gossip.

Your antics certainly dispel the stereotype that becoming a saint
is a grimly serious or lofty, otherworldly endeavor.

As I meditate on your life, St. Philip, I feel the need to examine
how active my sense of humor is in my pastoral efforts.

A sense of humor encompasses so many other qualities needed
in an effective priestly ministry.

A sense of humor includes open-mindedness,
genuine communication, deep respect for others,
the capacity to love and receive love with gratitude and joy,
self-control, openness to beauty, and realistic humility.

I think of Lyn Karol's quip, "Learn to laugh at your troubles
and you'll never run out of things to laugh at."

I think I can laugh at my own problems and troubles, St. Philip,
but it's altogether different when it comes to those of my people.
Perhaps this is where humor as a sense of balance comes in.
To look at another's trouble and find something positive in it
to balance what may well be that person's excruciating pain.

I'm convinced that a sense of humor with myself can be hope.
A sense of humor with others can be love.

Pray for me, St. Philip, that I may have this kind of humor
in my interactions with my people.

Then there is the story
of your mystical celebration of the Eucharist,
St. Philip.

This brings me face to face with an examination
of how I celebrate Eucharist.

It is so easy for me to slip into a routine,
not rattling through the words,
but perhaps not as conscious of the power of these words
as I should be.

I very much want to make my celebration of Eucharist
a mystical experience
and lead my people into this mystical experience of Jesus.

I sincerely believe that mystical experience
is not just for the chosen few.
Rather it is rooted in a keen awareness, in this case,
of the presence of Christ in the Eucharist and all this implies.

A mystical celebration of the Eucharist, St. Philip,
brings about and reinforces a personal inner unity
and a unification of the people with me and with one another.

A mystical celebration of Eucharist will empower our community
to go forth as the Body of Christ
to influence those in positions of decision-making
to make justice a reality for all with whom Jesus identifies himself.

St. Philip, I ask you, then, to obtain for me,
a priest striving to fulfill my vocation as well as I can,
a lively sense of humor and a spirit of mysticism.
Help me to blend them both in my loving service of my people
as you did in your priestly mission.

20

Peter Claver – Unveil Me

St. Peter Claver, your life is a living parable,
putting flesh on Jesus' words,
"Whatsoever you do for one of these, even the least. . . ."

Your missionary work among the slaves
in Cartagena in the Caribbean
challenges me to ask,
Who is the least in my priestly ministry?

St. Peter, the least might be that individual
who is always annoying me with scrupulous questions.
Or the least might be that member of the parish council
who is forever nit-picking and hair-splitting,
distracting everyone else from the business at hand.

Or the least might be that obnoxious glad-hander
who never tires of telling me
about all the important and influential people he knows.
Or the least might be that poor woman who has no clout,
who is in effect invisible,
whom I pass by with an absentminded nod of the head.
Or the least might be the person
who comes to the rectory without an appointment,
disturbing me from watching a sporting event on TV.
Or my secretary or the custodian or an altar server.

The least, St. Peter, are those I make the least.
Let a "heavy hitter" stop me and I give him my full attention.
The "most" are those who
because of money or power or influence
make me feel "less" and stoke my desire
to be accepted and appreciated
by the wealthy and powerful.

I ask you, St. Peter,
to help me to be more conscious of responding to these, the least,
as I would to Christ, just as you did.

What fascinates me about your work with the Caribbean slaves
is that you not only instructed and baptized
over three hundred thousand slaves
but you also brought them brandy and tobacco.

You were not only concerned
about their spiritual welfare, St. Peter,
but you also were absorbed in their physical needs.
And the brandy and tobacco are symbols of your caring
not just for their basic physical needs
but for their physical comfort and pleasure.

Sometimes I can be such a minimalist.
I do only what is demanded of me as a priest.
I don't walk that extra mile.
I'm too often satisfied with a mediocre response
to the needs of the people I serve.

I offer them the sacraments with a kind of punctilious ritualism
and call it quits.
Or I offer advice with a take-it-or-leave-it attitude,
not really getting involved in the person's pain or perplexity.

Help me, St. Peter, to see people as priceless individuals.
To see them as my sisters and brothers in Christ, as you did.

Aid me in realizing that I cannot truly care for each person
unless I know who each person is.
And that the people will not feel my concern
unless they know who I am.

Intercede for me, St. Peter, that I might reveal my true self
through my interactions with others,
letting them know where I am vulnerable
and where I am most alive.
Assist me to keep in mind that what I take time for
reveals my priorities.

Fortify me that I may be ever conscious
that the top of my priorities needs to be the fact
that those I might make the least
are the very ones I must give myself to the most.

Strengthen me, St. Peter, in my priestly dedication
not only to my people's spiritual development
but to their physical and social welfare as well.
Renew my fervor and always help me to do for others
what I would do for Jesus.

21

Margaret Mary Alacoque – Hearten Me

St. Margaret Mary, you were blessed with the grace to arouse in us the realization of God's love symbolized by the heart of Jesus.

I must admit that I haven't had that much devotion
to the Sacred Heart.

Yet when I think of the heart as the symbol of love,
I am attracted to meditating on divine love
—what it meant for you and what it means for me.

Divine love for you, St. Margaret Mary,
meant a great deal of suffering.

When I think of your own sisters' hostility toward you,
I feel embarrassed at the way I feel resentment
at the hurts inflicted on me.
I'm criticized and I sulk.
People disagree with me and I only want to avoid them.

Sometimes, St. Margaret Mary, I even question
why I ever became a priest
when I recall the way people
who are supposed to be a community of faith and love
can be so antagonistic, belligerent, and even hostile toward me.

What I experience is next to nothing
compared to what you had to suffer, St. Margaret Mary.
I wonder how I would have reacted to your revelations
were I your contemporary.
Probably I would have been as skeptical as those theologians
who called your visions delusions and told you to eat more heartily.

I know that I tend to draw back when people approach me
with some kind of message God was supposed to have given them.
I worry a lot about superstitious attitudes and practices.

Still you persevered in your love for the Heart of Jesus.

I meditate on your life, St. Margaret Mary,
and realize once again that life is not one long race
but many short races one after another.
Or as someone said, life by the yard is hard;
life by the inch is a cinch.

And isn't this what I should do in my priestly ministry: inch along?
Isn't this what Jesus' love challenges me to do?

If I preach to my people that they should forgive and forget,
isn't this what I should do
with those who seem to take delight in opposing my efforts?
Maybe there's just a little too much ego in my efforts and plans.
And the more ego there is, the less Jesus' love can get through to me
and through me to the people in my care.

I need to internalize your deathbed wish
to "lose myself in the heart of Jesus."

As a priest, St. Margaret Mary, I believe Jesus is using me
to reveal the love of his heart in such a way
that I can continually form the people I serve
into a community of authentic love.

Is there any better way to show forth the love of Jesus' heart
than to suffer patiently the wounds people inflict on me
just as you did?
Isn't this one way to lose myself in the heart of Jesus?

To lose myself in the heart of Jesus is not a matter of escapism,
hiding myself away from those who attack me.
Rather I go more deeply into Jesus' heart
in order to emerge and love my people,
especially those who oppose, confront, and resist me,
with the same kind of love with which Jesus loves me.

Isn't this what you did
even when parents of the children you taught
called you an imposter
and an unorthodox innovator,
St. Margaret Mary?
Isn't this what contributed so much to your becoming a saint?

St. Margaret Mary, intercede for me
that I may place my priestly heart within the Sacred Heart of Jesus
so that his love and my love may merge and become one love.
A love that forgives and reconciles,
a love that supports and affirms,
a love that sacrifices and exults.

22

Teresa of Avila – Mystic Me

What a glorious, wondrous, exciting saint you are, St. Teresa!

Your mysticism, your efforts at reform, your humor!
How attractive you are!

Your life and spirituality, St. Teresa, teach me
that mystical experience is not reserved for the chosen few.
It's for everyone.
Even for me as busy as I am in my priestly ministry.

There are times, I must admit,
when the yearning for the mystical
pulls me like a metal particle to a magnet.

But then I slip into the stereotype of mystics —
someone rapt in otherworldly contemplation,
her spirit ascending to heaven
like incense rising to the ceiling.
And I think, "This isn't for me."

However, you remind me, St. Teresa,
that the mystical experience is as much for me as it was for you.
Your writings on spirituality tell me that mystical experience
is the normal outgrowth of my prayer life.

So if I persist in thinking that mysticism isn't for me,
perhaps I should examine my prayer life.

How selfless is my prayer?
Or is my praying more autosuggestion
than an unselfish conversation with the God who dwells within me?
In other words, who is the center of my prayer?

I look to you, St. Teresa, for guidance in authentic praying
so that I won't be indulging in pompous fantasies,
comfortable coyness, or tinny sentimentalities.
In true prayer,
I need to be willing to suffer through the complexities of my life,
the quandaries of my interactions with my people,
the heartbreaks of my failures,
and the betrayals perpetrated against me.

I need to pray, St. Teresa,
with a creativity that pierces the mundane and finds the wondrous.
I need to heighten my tolerance for ambiguity,
realizing that praying is no guarantee
of clear-cut, black or white answers.

I want to pray, St. Teresa, in such a way
that my petitions are pledges of my action,
no matter what the cost
just as your prayer-life cost you so much opposition and turmoil
in your efforts to make your reforms a reality.

I want an ease in my prayer, St. Teresa,
with full knowledge that if I strain for results,
my prayer will end in ulcers and not in mystical experience.
I want to speak with Jesus with a friend-to-friend familiarity
as you did when you said,
"If this is the way you treat your friends,
no wonder you have so few."

Help me, dear St. Teresa,
so that my praying will be my opening to God dwelling within me.
Help me to make my praying my availability to God
so that God can do with me what he wills.

Help me to ponder the familiar until it becomes strange.
Help me to allow my prayer to be an expression of my uniqueness.

Never let me claim to be too busy to pray, St. Teresa.
Don't let me convince myself that mystical prayer is beyond me.
Help me to internalize your insight
that if we talk to God only on formal occasions,
soon we won't be talking to God at all.

Through your prayers for me, St. Teresa,
lead me to the conviction that mystical prayer
is as available to me as electricity is to a home.
But just as the amount of electricity I use
depends on the wattage of the light bulbs,
so too the amount of mysticism I experience
depends on how much of an authentic prayer life I have.

23

Kateri Tekakwitha – Prioritize Me

Blessed Kateri, your name means:
"She put things in order."

If there is one thing you can help me do
it is to put the busyness of my priestly days in order.
No matter how I try to map out my day,
there are so many interruptions that I never seem to be able
to get through my agenda.

There is a saying that my faith orders and directs my life
and makes it meaningful.
I pray, Blessed Kateri, for an increase of faith every day,
especially when I am preparing to celebrate Eucharist.

Sometimes I have difficulty
seeing the connection between my faith
and the chaos of my daily ministry.

Perhaps what I need to concentrate on, Blessed Kateri,
is the need to be more conscious of the possibility
that no matter how busy and distracted I become,
it is my faith that gives meaning to all I do.
I also need to find the unseen order in all that I do,
no matter how hectic things get.

There is, I believe, Blessed Kateri,
an unseen order in trying to see Christ coming to me
in each person who disrupts my tidy daily program.
There is also an unseen order
in my willingness to inconvenience myself
for the benefit of those who have no "appointment."

Despite your perennial weakness
from the small pox that had afflicted you, Blessed Kateri,
you worked hard in your village.
You lived up to your traditional Native American value
of working hard so that everyone could stay alive
and you believed firmly that your people came first.

This is the kind of order I need in my priestly ministry:
people come first.
It's so easy to get caught up in the "Kingdom of Thingdom."
Things and projects offer such unambiguous order.
I can look at my to-do list and cross each goal off
as I accomplish what *I* want to do.

But I have to have the faith that reminds me
that what I want to do with my day
may not be what God wants me to do.
People come first.
I must believe as with the same firm faith you had, Blessed Kateri,
that each person who comes into my life,
scheduled or disruptive,
has been sent to me by God.

Help me, Blessed Kateri,
to imitate your wonderful Native American spirituality
with its respect for all of creation
but most especially for those who have been created
in the image and likeness of God.

Help me to live your Native American insights like this one:
Whatever befalls the earth befalls the children of the earth;
we do not weave the web of life; we are merely a strand in it;
whatever we do to the web, we do to ourselves.

Help me, Blessed Kateri,
to put into practice another of your Native American values,
namely, kindness to strangers.
Intercede for me that I will always show kindness
to both strangers and the people I serve,
keeping in mind another of your Native American sayings:
This we know: the earth does not belong to the people;
people belong to the earth; all things are connected;
we are brothers and sisters.

Pray for me, Blessed Kateri,
that my faith will be reinforced so that I will be willing
to suffer inconvenience just as you suffered
for the Christian values of your new faith
which God gave you through the zealous Blackrobes
who worked among your people
back in the seventeenth century
in the area we now call New York.

24

Thomas Aquinas – Wonder Me

In these days of an unprecedented knowledge explosion,
St. Thomas,
and of a feverish exchange of information,
it's almost impossible to keep up.
Added to this the crushing demands made on my time,
I wonder just how I can find opportunities to read,
not to mention study.

Many times I just strike the pose
of intelligent reticence.
I do attend workshops,
but when the speaker talks to us,
I have this feeling I should already know
what he or she is telling me.

Then I ponder your life, St. Thomas,
and the glowing reports of your scholarship!
Of course, you were a monastic, I tell myself.
You didn't have people ringing your doorbell
or, more accurately,
pounding on your door all during each day.
You had the sumptuous preserve of silence
and holy segregation.

There was something a speaker said in one workshop:
"Knowledge comes by way of ignorance
so we should be encouraged by what we don't know."
Needless to say, St. Thomas, I have to feel most encouraged!

I have to admit that there are occasions
when I find it is difficult for me to find time
to prepare my weekend homilies.
That's how far my scholarship goes.

So, I pray to you, St. Thomas, asking you to help me
to have a sense of wonder in dealing with my people.
I ask for this because I know that I don't have to have
a great deal of knowledge to be filled with wonder.

For instance, I can stand under a star-studded sky
without knowing the names or positions of the stars
and overflow with wonder
at the immensity of the universe
and the fascinating wisdom
and lavish generosity of our Creator.

At the same time I don't want to use a sense of wonder as an excuse
for not finding out the names of at least some of the stars
— an excuse for not pursuing knowledge.
I accede to the insight that
in wonder all wisdom begins,
in wonder all wisdom ends,
but the first wonder is the offspring of ignorance,
the second wonder is the parent of knowledge.

I also ask you, St. Thomas,
to help me to use whatever knowledge I do have
to be wise in serving my people.
As the poet Tennyson once penned,
"Knowledge comes but wisdom lingers."

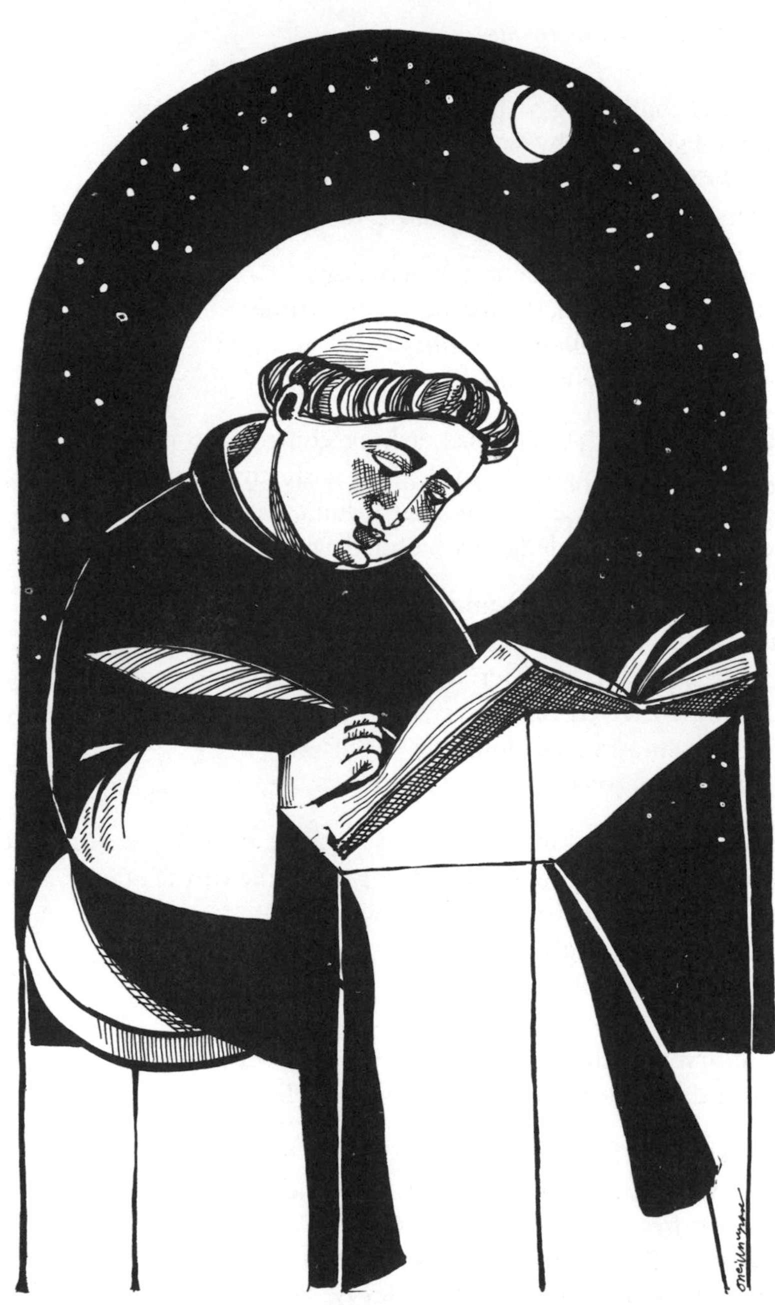

In working with the people God has given me to serve,
I want especially the wisdom
of knowing what to overlook.
The wisdom of giving others
the benefit of the doubt.

Without this kind of wisdom,
I could take a nosedive into self-righteous judgmentalism.
This is easy enough to do
when I'm confronted almost constantly
with the faults and shortcomings of people.
I need wisdom to be keenly aware that we are all human
therefore limited therefore imperfect.

If wisdom is knowledge that knows its limits, St. Thomas,
I should be most wise.
There is an adage that fits in here:
The wise know that they know little.

I especially need the wisdom that comes from learning
from my own shortcomings and mistakes.

I think of the Wise Men
who visited Jesus with their gifts
and recognize that the truly generous are the truly wise.
Like those Wise Men
who saw through a child to God,
I know that human insights
are flashes of divine wisdom.
And this, St. Thomas, is what I need.

Just as I can see the infinite Creator in a starry sky,
so too I need to be able to see Christ
in each person who comes to me.
I need to see through the dreary routines of my daily ministry
to my involvement in continuing Jesus' saving action in history.

As the poet Emerson wrote,
"The invariable mark of wisdom
is to see the miraculous in the common."

And in the end, St. Thomas,
I ask you to intercede for me
that God will increase my wisdom
so that I will make time for study,
so that I will not grow stale in offering my people God's word,
so that I will be a competent presenter of divine mysteries.

Unlike those who lecture us at our workshops
in order to inform us,
I want to preach in order to inspire my people,
to move them to a desire to better themselves
in all areas of their lives and relationships
for the glory of God.

I come to you, Angelic Doctor,
asking you to intercede for me
that I may be worthy of my calling,
especially that of sharing the Word with my people.
I don't ask that you supply what I don't know,
but that you guide me into making the effort
to know what I don't know
and to seek further knowledge for the glory of God
and the benefit of my people, as you did.

25

Francis de Sales – Gentle Me

St. Francis, you are a very attractive personality.
Perhaps it's because of your sense of balance.

In your work *An Introduction to the Devout Life*
you don't go to extremes counseling people to forsake the world
in order to become saints.

You maintain that everyone should strive for holiness
and that it is not only an error, but even a heresy,
to hold that sanctity is incompatible with any state of life.

Despite your statement
as clear as a note from a Stradivarius, St. Francis,
the laity have been and in some areas still are regarded
as second-class citizens within the church.

Your work is a masterpiece of psychology,
practical morality, and common sense.
This is what I find so attractive.

Yet with all your balance and gentleness,
I recall that under your episcopal robes you wore a hair shirt.

What an example you set for me, St. Francis,
as I go about my days of priestly ministry:

balance and gentleness in dealing with my people
and a spirit of penance in my own life.

St. Francis, to be balanced and gentle,
I need to be patient with others
and give them the benefit of the doubt in all circumstances.
I have to be on guard against all tendencies to judge others rashly,
based only on appearances without sufficient evidence.

I need to live the insight
that just because someone does something evil
doesn't mean that that person *is* evil.
Someone might commit the sin of theft
but that doesn't mean that person *is* a thief.

While giving others the benefit of the doubt, St. Francis,
I shouldn't take it easy on myself,
allow myself to slip into mindless complacency,
become satisfied with blissful mediocrity.

I need a spirit of penance like you had,
St. Francis, especially for my sins of omission.

The many times when I could have given more of myself
to someone in need of my gentle listening
and instead glanced at my watch,
hoping I could get to see the last quarter of a game.

Or the times when I've cut someone off
in the middle of that person's recital of a problem
with quick-fix advice.

Or the times when I've told someone I was too busy
when I wasn't.

There are many more sins of omission I'm guilty of
and so I need to do penance for them.

Perhaps I won't wear a hair shirt as you did, St. Francis,
but there are other forms of penance I can do.

I can inconvenience myself more and with a joyful spirit.
I can spend more quality time preparing my homilies.
I can pay more attention to an aged person who is just rambling.

These and other acts of penance can be my hair shirt.

So I ask you, St. Francis, to help me in my priestly ministry
to be realistic in encouraging my people to strive after sanctity.
To be much more respectful of their lifestyles, their struggles,
their heartbreaks, their burdens, their hopes,
their aspirations, their goals.

Let me learn the true spirit
of penitential sacrifice from them, St. Francis.
From a mother who paces the midnight floor
clutching a sick baby in her arms.
From a son who leaves his day's work
only to go home and care so carefully for an aged mother
day after day.
From a father whose wife died suddenly
and who is doing his best to raise two small children.

Second-raters? Never.
And I thank you, St. Francis, for reminding me.

26

Ignatius of Loyola – Nonviolence Me

In these days of rampant, random, casual violence,
you, St. Ignatius, stand out as clear as sunlight in the summer,
as solid as a mountain, for pacifism.

Granted you were wounded in battle,
but you made a conscious choice to give up your career as a soldier
and opted for the work of peacemaking.

In my ministry as a priest, St. Ignatius,
as in the ministries of all the People of God,
I think the most important work I can do
is that of being peacemaker.

My people and I gather as a worshiping community of faith,
recite the responses, sing the hymns, receive Jesus in the Eucharist.
And we also exchange some sign of peace!

As I stand at the altar, St. Ignatius,
I am aware that what we as a community desperately need
is to put that sign of peace into action.
We need to be a community of nonviolence.
But I am also aware that I can lead
these sincerely worshiping people in front of me to nonviolence
only if I have this quality in myself.

It is so easy, St. Ignatius,
for me to stand and expound in my homilies
the need for peacemaking to counteract the violence in our culture.
But I am challenged to examine myself
to discover whether or not I am genuinely nonviolent,
whether or not I am an authentic peacemaker.

And I must be ruthlessly honest with myself about myself.

And here is where you come in, St. Ignatius.
Your Spiritual Exercises help me to understand
that I can't be truly honest about myself
without a systematic, regularly scheduled, relevant, self-searching,
community-validated approach to my spiritual development.

There is an insight in John Shea's book *Gospel Light*
that "if we follow spiritual exercises,
certain inner spaces will open,
certain realizations will occur,
certain levels of consciousness will develop."

And I am convinced, St. Ignatius, that in those opened spaces,
newer realizations, and higher levels of consciousness,
I will be able to evaluate myself honestly as a peacemaker.

There is the obvious violence like abortion,
physician-assisted suicide, drive-by killings.

There is overt racial violence,
which is not the preserve of the KKK
but also of more ordinary people.
There may not be that many cross-burnings,
but there is arson, assault, murder, shootings,
bombings, harassment of ethnic groups:
African Americans, Jews, Hispanics, Asians, Arabs.

But there is a more subtle kind of violence
that I must inspire my people to counteract
with their peacemaking efforts.

There is a kind of violence in advertising
that appeals successfully to people's deep-seated search for freedom
with promises of all kinds of license.

For example, there is a kind of violence
in the advertised promises of freedom from bad breath, from zits,
from overweight, from debt, from sexual inhibition,
from personal responsibility for our own actions
and for the decisions and actions of elected officials,
from illness, from psychological neurosis, from cultural mores,
from social unacceptability.

There is violence in the obscene salaries
corporate presidents and professional athletes receive
while eight hundred children under the age of one die each day
from malnutrition or starvation *in the United States!*

And perhaps the worst violence of all is that our culture
lives in a la-la land of material comfort for the upwardly mobile
as though ignoring the problems of the poor and discarded
will make those problems disappear.

It is into this world, St. Ignatius,
that I must go with the healing of my priestly ministry,
persuasively leading my people.
I need to be fearless as I try to cope with the built-in tension
between peacemakers and power-mongers.

I call upon you, St. Ignatius, to intercede for me
that I will have the courage and honesty I need
to be a Christ-like peacemaker
and a model of nonviolence for my people.

27

Clare – Determine Me

One thing that attracts me to you, St. Clare,
is your friendship with Francis of Assisi.

So often, if not always,
when a priest has a friendship with a woman,
it is as suspect as an ex-con hanging around a bank.

We hear so much today about men,
especially priests maybe,
getting in touch with their feminine side.
And rightly so.
Often, perhaps too often, priests,
with their promise of celibacy or vow of chastity,
end up being self-centered, even frigid, bachelors.

Sometimes, St. Clare, the warmth of first fervor
freezes into icy isolation over the years.
The outgoing sensitivity
that made us newly ordained priests so attractive
tightens into a knot of self-preoccupation.
Often these changes happen
because of a lack of human affection in our lives
without our realizing it.

Because of your friendship with Francis, St. Clare,
I believe that friendships with women
can help me to enhance my sensitivity and empathy.

I also believe that when priests and women are involved
in healthy, creative, life-giving friendships,
they can challenge each other
to continued fuller and more holistic growth and development
while they strengthen one another's
male and female significant qualities.

Your friendship with Francis reminds me
of what Gibran said about relationships,
"Stand together but not too near;
the oak and cypress don't grow in each other's shadow."
Francis was your mentor,
but you flourished in your own kind of spirituality.

The characteristics I most admire about you, St. Clare,
are your determination and commitment.

When your parents tried forcibly
to turn you away from the path of spirituality you chose,
you remained firm like a rock in floodwaters.

These are the virtues I need to be renewed in:
determination and commitment.
And I call upon your intercession, St. Clare,
to help me to develop them more and more
in my priestly ministry.

I especially need to be determined and committed
to a more self-revealing communication, St. Clare.
A communication which enables me to open myself up
and allow the real me rather than the role me
to be seen and touched, interacted with and savored.

I believe, as someone pointed out,
that when I really commit myself to authentic communicating,
intimacy is inevitable.

Far from using my celibacy as an escape from intimacy,
please help me, St. Clare,
to have the courage to nurture and appreciate
the gifts of love and warmth offered to me,
especially from women.

I want this warm and loving friendship from women
to open up for me the possibility
of getting in touch with my feminine side
by feeling more empathetically,
putting myself more compassionately in another's place,
seeing things more responsively from another's point of view;
by listening more in a nurturing way,
actually hearing what people are saying
rather than being too analytical;
by being more open and accepting,
allowing others to express their emotions and feelings
without being too quick with observations and advice.

It's a big order, I know.
But with your help, St. Clare, I am convinced
that I can grow more fully,
become more wholly myself.
Please intercede for me, St. Clare,
that through my holistic development,
I may empower the people I am serving
to allow the warmth and trust of their affection
to grow and be shared
with unselfconscious joy and unashamed candor.

28

Catherine of Siena – Self-Knowledge Me

According to *The Catholic Encyclopedia,* St. Catherine,
"The key-note to your teaching is that we,
whether in the cloister or in the world,
must ever abide in the cell of self-knowledge."

What an awe-inspiring summation of your life and teachings.

I am certainly a priest "in the world," not in a cloister.
Yet, according to your teaching, St. Catherine,
I am just as obliged to follow the rough road
of introspection that leads to self-knowledge
as anyone in a cloister.

There is a line from the mystic Meister Eckhart,
"No one has known God who has not known himself."

It's an interesting insight.
Meister Eckhart seems to be saying
we need to know ourselves first
and then proceed to knowing God.
So often we begin with knowledge of God
and then we proceed to self-knowledge.
Often we stop short at our knowledge of God
and never bother with self-knowledge.

Perhaps, St. Catherine, this is one of the reasons
why people can be so smug in their piety
and yet be so psychologically off balance.
They say they put all their trust in God
but they can't trust their own intuitions and appraisals.
Like a trapeze artist, they walk the tightrope
between security in their piety and emotional instability.

Perhaps as seminarians, we should have had
four years of psychology in conjunction with theology
since many of our well-intentioned people
have serious to surface psychological problems
that are masked as spiritual enigmas.

In my own case, St. Catherine, I recognize my need
for a spirituality that is rooted in self-knowledge.
I need a self-knowledge that will empower me
to evaluate myself in an honest, balanced way.
I need self-knowledge not only to discover my weaknesses
which allow me to water down Jesus' teachings
but also to discern my many qualities
that enable me to put Jesus' teachings
into interpersonal practice.

I must make my spirituality, like yours, St. Catherine,
one that finds security in my failings
because I believe God is infinitely merciful.
And also in my strengths
because all that I am and can become
is God's gift to me.

As a priest, St. Catherine, I can pose,
but for my spirituality to be authentic,
I need to be at all times and under all circumstances
my real self, warts and all.

Whether I am revealing my frailties or my strengths,
I must be comfortable in knowing
that I am divulging my real me.

Too many are spiritually schizophrenic:
they are confident when dealing with God
but insecure when assessing themselves.
They can spiel off many learned facts about God
but they only stammer in pathetic embarrassment
when they speak of themselves.

Yet I know, St. Catherine, that before God
I must strip myself of all masks and camouflages.
As the Psalmist sang,
"Lord, you have probed me, you know me:
you know when I sit and stand;
you understand my thoughts from afar."

And the beauty of your teaching, St. Catherine,
is that God wants me and all of us
to know ourselves in the same way:
totally, thoroughly, absolutely, accurately,
definitively, favorably and unfavorably.

Help me, St. Catherine, to know and love myself
in an emotionally and psychologically healthy way
that I may know and love God authentically as a whole person.

29

Martín de Porres — All-Inclusive Me

It breaks my heart, St. Martin,
when I read that your father, a white noble Spaniard,
hated you and your sister because your skin pigmentation
resembled that of your mother, a Panamanian.
Just as heartbreaking is the fact that you and your sister
were both illegitimate.

As I look for something
I can use from your life in my priestly ministry,
I am immediately confronted with the sin of racism.
The sin that maintains that race determines inherently
the superiority of a particular race
—and the inferiority of another!

There was a question raised by an African American
that went like this:
Do you know how it feels
to have people cross the street to get away from you?
to have a security guard follow you around a store?
to have women clutch their purses to their chests when they see you?
Well, that's how it is to be young and black.

I don't even have to go into the atrocious sin of slavery,
the godless blight on our nation's history.

But what does distress and perturb me
is how today so-called white people
dismiss that blasphemous chapter in our history
by saying things like, "That was then, this is now."
Or, "Sure, their ancestors were slaves, but they're not."

How easily we fall into the trap of revisionist history.
How comfortably we sanitize the sin of racism
with a phrase like "racial tensions."

On the other hand, St. Martin,
I will never forget how a whole nation
was riveted to the TV
during the showing of *Roots*.

However, it seems to me, St. Martin,
that having watched that production
and sympathizing with the inhumane conditions
and the sadistic suffering of slaves
inflicted by those who were enslaved
in their own slick superiority,
many viewers thought that this exonerated them
from any further consideration or examination
of the racist attitude that continues to these days.
And the sin of racism is not confined
to our bigotry against African Americans.
Bigotry includes Jews, Hispanics, Asians, Arabs, homosexuals
—and Catholics!

But what really agitates me, St. Martin,
is the probability that many fervent, righteous
church-going Christians
don't even think of racism as a sin.

But racism doesn't just exist in the moral order.
Bigotry is the offspring of ignorance.

As one writer put it:
More evil has come into the world from ignorance
than from people who have sinned or made mistakes.

It is ignorance, St. Martin, that induces people
to judge a whole group by several members of that group.

I hear it: "You know how those people are."

I have no doubt that those who haughtily look down on
and scurrilously put down others
do so because of their own lack of self-worth and self-acceptance.
There are those who are bigoted racially and in other ways
because of their dire need to exalt themselves
by humiliating and degrading others.

If there is one fact known
from even a cursory glance at the gospel, St. Martin, it is this:
Christ came to break down the walls of division
and to melt the iron bars of bigotry.
He prayed "that they all may be one as you, Father, and I are one."
He called us, his followers, the "branches," united to him, the Vine.
St. Paul called this unity Christ's Body with Christ as the Head.

There can be no justification, St. Martin,
for the simplistic adherence to extreme positions
or even the slightest hint of racial bigotry among Christ's followers,
if they are true, genuine, authentic disciples of the One who said,
"I am the Way, I am the Truth."

Jesus' love is all-inclusive.
Can my love or my people's love be less?

And I, St. Martin, as a priest of Jesus who is the Way,
must do all in my power to lead my people
to an all-embracing attitude and behavior toward all people.

As a priest of Jesus who is the Light,
I must do everything I can to heal jaundiced eyes.

This means, St. Martin,
that I have to see each person as priceless in the sight of God,
uniquely created in his image and likeness.
I must also see Christ in each person and conduct myself
with the same heartfelt, self-sacrificing, affirming respect
toward each person as I would toward Christ.

Pray for me, St. Martin,
that I will always be open and receptive to all people,
no matter what their race or nationality or skin color
or religious orientation or needs.

Help me to let the door of my heart
stand wide open to everyone without judgment
and accept people as they are and as they can become,
open especially to those whose voices I'd rather not hear.

Help me and the people I serve, St. Martin,
to be like lines that lead to the center of a circle, uniting there,
and not like parallel lines that never touch.

Intercede for me that I, a priest, will be a truly Christ-like
leader of the kind of worshiping faith community
in which a sense of belonging, of being known,
loved, cared for, and challenged
will always prevail
for everyone without exception.

30

Hyacintha Mariscotti – Recommitment Me

As I ponder your life, St. Hyacintha,
I realize my need
for continual conversion and recommitment.

One of the built-in assumptions in my life as a priest
is that at ordination I made my commitment
and it was once and done.
As a result,
I also may assume that my conversion to Christ
was and is total and absolute.

But your life, St. Hyacintha,
underscores the lie of these assumptions.

Because your younger sister
was married before you were,
you made life intolerable for everyone in your family,
so much so that your father shipped you off
to a Franciscan convent.

It would have been a wondrous story of piety
if it read that there, in that convent,
you gave yourself entirely to God
and became a model of virtue and holiness.

But that wasn't the way it was.
Having arrived at the convent
you proceeded to live a life of epicurean luxury
that scandalized all the other sisters
and caused them turmoil beyond description.
And you lived this opulent life for ten long years!

But because your father subsidized the convent,
the sisters were helpless, trapped.
You did everything you could
to make their lives as miserable as yours.
They had to bear their cross — and you were their cross.

But then there came the day of grace in disguise.
You were struck down with a serious illness.
At first, you reacted as you always did
when things didn't go your way:
you were indignant, miserable, outraged, and furious.

The sisters' cross weighed heavier.
It became a torturous crucifix.

But then — and there are no details here — you changed.
The suffering you experienced in your illness
became the grace of your conversion.
You rose out of your sick bed
and became a model of self-discipline and charity.

At first the sisters were excusably skeptical.
But as time went on and you continued to grow in holiness,
the sisters could do only one thing: emulate you.

Yours, St. Hyacintha, is a fascinating story of conversion:
of petulance converted to humility,
of self-centeredness converted to gracious service,
of sumptuous living converted to a true spirit of poverty.

As I contemplate your life story, St. Hyacintha,
I realize that conversion which does not disrupt a lifestyle
serves only as a comfort to the converted.
Conversion that does not bring about radical change for the better
will never lead to recommitment.

These insights are urgently important for me in my priestly ministry.
Again, there is another built-in assumption I have to deal with:
that there is an inherent holiness in being a priest.

If I live that assumption, I will never enter into
the many conversions and recommitments I must experience
if I am to grow in genuine holiness.
Rather, I will live a life of haughty presumption — a sin against hope.

What your life teaches me, St. Hyacintha,
is that there must always be hope for a change for the better,
hope that I can be holier,
hope that I can become a saint as you did
through my many conversions and recommitments.

I also learn from your life, St. Hyacintha,
that to be truly converted and recommitted
I must deal with my Shadow Self.

I know, according to the famous psychiatrist Carl Jung
that in me and in the people I serve, there is a Shadow Self.
The Shadow Self is a hiding place for those things about myself
I don't want to face or can't live with.
The Shadow Self is a kind of burial ground
where I entomb my unacceptable character flaws.
But I bury them alive.
And because I have not dealt with
the detestable aspects of my personality,
they rise from the burial ground to haunt and depress me
and make me feel miserable and worthless.

Unacceptable character flaws that spill over
into the lives of those I should be serving with Christ-like fervor,
like my violence against others
which I justify as doing good for them.
My petty selfishness that I disguise as personal security.
My acid cynicism toward human weakness that I call being realistic.

The fact that I won't call my vices by their proper names
only proves that I am living in darkness,
that I am preventing the Light who is Christ
from shining into my Shadow Self.

My Shadow Self is that part of me that is so detestable
that I don't even want to admit it exists.
But it does.
And it is the scum and bilge of my Shadow Self,
which I refuse to cleanse from myself,
that prevents me from being converted and recommitted
to the goal of becoming a saintly priest.

But your life story, St. Hyacintha, gives me hope.
The hope that I can always change and change many times
for the better, for the best.

Help me, St. Hyacintha, to live the words of Cardinal Newman:
"To live is to change and to be perfect is to have changed often."

Help me to rise out of my Shadow Self
and enter into the light of conversion and recommitment
just as you rose out of your sick bed to become a saint.